Hitting America's Soft Underbelly

The Potential Threat of Deliberate Biological Attacks Against the U.S. Agricultural and Food Industry

T0162207

PETER CHALK

Prepared for the Office of the Secretary of Defense
Approved for public release, distribution unlimited

NATIONAL DEFENSE RESEARCH INSTITUTE

The research described in this report was sponsored by the Office of the Secretary of Defense (OSD). The research was conducted in the RAND National Defense Research Institute, a federally funded research and development center supported by the OSD, the Joint Staff, the unified commands, and the defense agencies under Contract DASW01-01-C-0004.

Library of Congress Cataloging-in-Publication Data

Chalk, Peter.
    Hitting America's soft underbelly : the potential threat of deliberate biological attacks against the U.S. agricultural and food industry / Peter Chalk.
      p. cm.
    Includes bibliographical references.
    "MG-135."
    ISBN 0-8330-3522-3 (pbk. : alk. paper)
    1. Agriculture—Defense measures—United States. 2. Civil defense—United States. 3. Food industry and trade—Defense measures—United States. 4. Bioterrorism—United States—Prevention. I. Title.

UA929.95.A35C49 2004
363.32—dc22

                        2003026834

The RAND Corporation is a nonprofit research organization providing objective analysis and effective solutions that address the challenges facing the public and private sectors around the world. RAND's publications do not necessarily reflect the opinions of its research clients and sponsors.

RAND® is a registered trademark.

Published 2004 by the RAND Corporation
1700 Main Street, P.O. Box 2138, Santa Monica, CA 90407-2138
1200 South Hayes Street, Arlington, VA 22202-5050
201 North Craig Street, Suite 202, Pittsburgh, PA 15213-1516
RAND URL: http://www.rand.org/
To order RAND documents or to obtain additional information, contact
Distribution Services: Telephone: (310) 451-7002;
Fax: (310) 451-6915; Email: order@rand.org

Preface

Over the past decade, the United States has endeavored to increase its ability to detect, prevent, and respond to terrorist threats and incidents. This focus on protecting the country from attacks, which has involved considerable financial outlays, has contributed to an increasingly well-protected public infrastructure. Critical to this endeavor has been the development of vulnerability-threat analyses that are designed to maximize both antiterrorist efforts and consequence management procedures. Agriculture, however, has received comparatively little attention with respect to protection against terrorist incidents. In terms of accurate threat assessments and consequence management procedures, the agriculture sector, and the food industry in general, by and large has not been a part of the wide-ranging emphasis that has been given to critical infrastructure protection in the United States.

This report aims to expand the current debate on domestic homeland security by assessing the vulnerabilities of the agricultural sector and the food chain to a deliberate act of biological terrorism. The report begins with a discussion of the methods used to conduct the analysis and the current state of research on threats to agricultural livestock and produce. It then outlines agriculture's importance to the U.S. economy, assesses the vulnerabilities in the general food industry, examines the capabilities that are needed to exploit those vulnerabilities, and explores the likely outcomes from a successful attack. The report next considers the question of why terrorists have yet to employ agricultural assaults as a method of operation and concludes with proposed recommendations for the U.S. policymaking community.

The study should be of interest to policymakers concerned with issues related to U.S. homeland security, critical infrastructure protection, and possible future terrorist uses of biological agents.

Research for this report was conducted within the Federal Research Program, International Security and Defense Policy Center of the RAND National Security Research Division (NSRD). NSRD conducts research and analysis for a broad range of clients, including the U.S. Department of Defense, allied foreign governments, the intelligence community, and foundations.

Contents

Tables

Summary

The Importance of the U.S. Agricultural Industry and Its Vulnerability to Disruption

Agriculture[1] and the food industry in general are enormously important to the social, economic, and, arguably, political stability of the United States. Although farming directly employs less than 3 percent of the American population, one in eight people works in an occupation that is directly supported by food production. Agriculture's share of produce sold overseas is more than double that of other U.S. industries, which makes the sector a major component in the U.S. balance of trade.

Unfortunately, the agriculture and food industries are vulnerable to deliberate (and accidental) disruption. Critical concerns in this area include:

- The concentrated and intensive nature of contemporary U.S. farming practices
- The increased susceptibility of livestock to disease
- A general lack of farm/food-related security and surveillance
- An inefficient, passive disease-reporting system that is further hampered by a lack of trust between regulators and producers
- Veterinarian training that tends not to emphasize foreign animal diseases (FADs) or large-scale husbandry

---

[1] For the purposes of this report, *agriculture* refers to all activities included in the production cycle of the entire food industry. Wholesalers and restaurant chains are included as related entities that are directly dependent on the agriculture industry; they occupy the "supply" end of the farm-to-table continuum.

- A prevailing focus on aggregate, rather than individual, livestock statistics

Although vulnerability does not equate to risk, and there are few recorded instances of terrorists actually using disease against agriculture, a realistic potential for disruption exists. Indeed, what makes the vulnerabilities inherent in agriculture so worrying is that the capability requirements for exploiting those weaknesses are not significant and are certainly less considerable than those needed for a human-directed bio-attack.

Several factors account for this situation. First, there is a large menu of agents from which to choose, with no less than 15 "List A" pathogens identified by the Office International des Epizooties (OIE) as having the potential to severely effect agricultural populations and/or trade. Most of these diseases are environmentally hardy—being able to exist for extended periods of time on organic or inorganic matter—and typically are not the focus of concerted livestock vaccination programs in the United States.

Second, many FADs are *non-zoonotic*, meaning they cannot "jump" the animal-human species barrier; as such, there is no risk of latent or accidental (human) infection associated with these pathogens. Thus, the perpetrator is not required to have an advanced understanding of animal disease epidemiology and transmission modes, nor is there any need for elaborate containment procedures, personal protective equipment, and/or prophylaxis antibiotics in the preparation of the disease agent.

Third, animal diseases can be quickly spread to affect large numbers of herds over wide geographic areas. This factor reflects the intensive and concentrated nature of modern farming practices in the United States and the increased susceptibility of livestock to viral and bacterial infections. There is, in other words, no issue of weaponization that needs to be addressed in agricultural terrorism because the animals themselves are the primary vector for pathogenic transmission.

Fourth, if the objective is human deaths, the food chain offers a low-tech mechanism that is nevertheless conducive to disseminating toxins and bacteria. Developments in the farm-to-table food continuum have greatly increased the number of entry points for these agents. These openings for contaminants combined with the lack of security and surveillance at many processing and packing plants, have helped to substantially augment the technical ease of orchestrating a food-borne attack.

The Impact of a Major Act of Agroterrorism

The impact of a major agricultural/food-related disaster in the United States would be significant and could easily extend beyond the agricultural community to affect other segments of society.

Perhaps one of the most immediate effects of a major act of biological agroterrorism[2] would be economic disruption, generating costs on at least three different levels. First, there would be direct losses resulting from containment measures and the destruction of disease-ridden livestock. Second, indirect multiplier effects would accrue from compensation costs paid to farmers for the destruction of agricultural commodities and losses suffered by both directly and indirectly related industries. Finally, international costs would accumulate in the form of protective trade embargoes imposed by major external trading partners.

A successful act of agroterrorism could also undermine the domestic confidence in and support of government. The release of contagious pathogens against livestock or the contamination of the farm-to-table continuum through the introduction of toxic or bacterial agents could cause the public to question the safety of the food supply and lead to speculation about the effectiveness of existing contingency planning against weapons of mass destruction in general.

---

[2] For the purposes of this report, *agroterrorism* is defined as the deliberate introduction of a disease agent, either against livestock or into the food chain, for purposes of undermining socioeconomic stability and/or generating fear. Depending on the disease agent and pathogenic vector chosen, agroterrorism is a tactic that can be used either to cause mass socioeconomic disruption or as a form of direct human aggression.

The mechanics of dealing with a major act of agroterrorism could trigger additional public criticism. Mass eradication and disposal of livestock in particular could be controversial, possibly eliciting protests from affected farmers and animal rights and environmental groups.

Beyond their immediate economic and political impact, bioterrorist assaults against agriculture and/or the food chain have the potential to create social panic. Attacks that have a direct impact on public health by causing human deaths and injuries could be expected to have particularly unsettling effects. Terrorists could use the resulting fear and alarm to their advantage to create an overall atmosphere of anxiety without actually having to carry out indiscriminate civilian-directed attacks.

Policy Recommendations

The United States, more by luck than by design, has not experienced the type of major agricultural or food-related disasters to which other countries and polities, such as the United Kingdom, Malaysia, and Taiwan, have been subjected in recent years. As a result, there is no widespread recognition of either the potential threat or the consequences of such an event taking place on American soil.

The United States ignores the continuing vulnerability of the agricultural sector at its own peril. Policy reforms can, and indeed should, be instituted to pursue a more aggressive and coordinated strategy to secure the industry against deliberate attack. Such measures would have the ancillary benefit of augmenting overall response and consequence-management efforts for dealing with naturally occurring outbreaks of food contamination or disease in livestock. These initiatives should (1) build on programs already under way; (2) leverage existing federal, state, and local capabilities; and (3) involve key customers, stakeholders, and partners.

At least six policy recommendations can be made for the short and medium term:

- First, a comprehensive needs analysis should be undertaken to ascertain appropriate investment requirements for the federal emergency management infrastructure.
- Second, a move must be made to increase the number of state and local personnel who have the requisite skills to identify and treat exotic FADs.
- Third, assessments of how to foster more-coordinated and standardized links between the U.S. agricultural and intelligence communities should be undertaken.
- Fourth, attention needs to be directed to issues of law enforcement and the use of forensic investigations to determine whether disease outbreaks have been deliberately orchestrated or are the result of naturally occurring phenomena.
- Fifth, the overall effectiveness of the passive (i.e., voluntary) disease reporting system needs to be revisited, especially in relation to providing more consistency with indemnity payments to compensate farmers for destroyed livestock and improving the effectiveness of communication channels between agricultural producers and regulators.
- Finally, surveillance, internal quality control, and emergency response at food processing and packing plants need to be addressed and evaluated to weigh the immediate costs of improving biosecurity against the long-term benefits of instituting those upgrades.

Over the longer term, additional effort should be directed toward standardizing and streamlining food supply and agricultural safety measures within the framework of a single, integrated strategy that cuts across the missions and capabilities of federal, state, and local agencies. An effort such as this would help to unify the patchwork of largely uncoordinated bio-emergency preparedness and response initiatives that presently exists in the United States. Integration of agriculture and food safety measures would also serve to reduce jurisdictional conflicts and eliminate unnecessary duplication of effort.

Acknowledgments

The author wishes to express his thanks to all those who made this research possible. I would especially like to acknowledge officials and academics with the Agricultural Research Service (ARS), the Animal and Plant Health Inspection Service (APHIS), the Food Safety Inspection Service (FSIS), the California Department of Food and Agriculture (CDFA), and the University of California, Davis, who were willing to be interviewed for this study and who provided invaluable background material and commentaries on the structure and vulnerability of the U.S. agricultural sector. (Names of individuals have been deliberately omitted for purposes of confidentiality.)

A special debt of appreciation is also owed to Jack Riley, director of RAND's Public Safety and Justice research unit, and Terry Wilson, animal disease specialist with the U.S. Army Medical Research Institute of Infectious Diseases at Fort Detrick in Frederick, Maryland, both of whom provided highly useful and insightful comments on the draft version of this study.

Finally, I would like to thank RAND's NSRD for its interest and assistance in funding this study and the editor, Nancy DelFavero, for all of her help on the final report.

Needless to say, any errors and omissions are the sole responsibility of the author.

Acronyms

AHS	African horse sickness (virus)
AI	avian influenza
APHIS	Animal and Plant Health Inspection Service
ARS	Agriculture Research Service
ASF	African swine fever
BSL	biosafety level
BT	Bluetongue (virus)
BTWC	Biological and Toxin Weapons Convention
BW	biological weapon
CDFA	California Department of Food and Agriculture
CIA	Central Intelligence Agency
CIP	critical infrastructure protection
DIA	Defense Intelligence Agency
END	Exotic Newcastle Disease
ESA	Emergency Supplementary Assistance
FAD	foreign animal disease
FBI	Federal Bureau of Investigation
FMD	foot and mouth disease
FSIS	Food Safety and Inspection Services
FY	fiscal year

GAO	General Accounting Office
GDP	gross domestic product
HACCP	Hazard Analysis and Critical Control Points
LSD	Lumpy skin disease (virus)
OIE	Office International des Epizooties
PDD	Presidential Decision Directive
PPE	personal protective equipment
RP	Rinderpest (virus)
RVF	Rift Valley fever
SGP	sheep and goat pox (viruses)
SVD	Swine vesicular disease
UK	United Kingdom
USDA	U.S. Department of Agriculture
VS	vesicular stomatitis
WNV	West Nile Virus

CHAPTER ONE

Introduction

Over the past decade, the United States has endeavored to increase its ability to detect, prevent, and respond to terrorist threats and incidents. Much of this focus on augmenting homeland security, which has involved considerable financial outlays, has been aimed at upgrading the public infrastructure through the development of vulnerability threat analyses designed to maximize both anti-terrorism and consequence management efforts.

Although many gaps remain in the United States government's overall strategy to mitigate domestic terrorism in the country, investments in incident preparedness, training, and response have contributed to the development of at least basic emergency management command structures. These nascent efforts have incrementally addressed the scope of potential terrorist attacks, from conventional bombings to more "exotic" biological, chemical, radiological, and nuclear incidents.

Agriculture[1] and food production and supply, however, are industries that have received comparatively little attention in the general field of counterterrorism and homeland security. In terms of accurate threat assessments and consequence management procedures, the agricultural sector is somewhat of a latecomer to the growing emphasis on critical infrastructure protection (CIP) in the United States. Indeed, agriculture was not originally included under the provisions

---

[1] For the purposes of this report, *agriculture* refers to all activities included in the production cycle of the entire food industry. Wholesalers and restaurant chains are included as related entities that are directly dependent on the agriculture industry; they occupy the "supply" end of the farm-to-table continuum.

of Presidential Decision Directive 63 (PDD-63), which specifies critical "nodes" (i.e., systems) deemed to be vulnerable to terrorist attack or disruption, and was incorporated as a specific component of U.S. national counterterrorist strategy only after the September 11 attacks on the Pentagon and World Trade Center in 2001.[2]

Research Methods

The research for this study proceeded in five main stages:

First, a qualitative and conceptual framework for analyzing threats to agriculture and the food chain in general was created, based primarily on the author's subject matter background and previous writings.[3]

Second, interviews were conducted with members of the U.S. policy community to determine the specific makeup of the American farm-to-table food continuum, the extent of agriculture's interface with current developments in national critical infrastructure protec-

---

[2] In May 1998, the Clinton administration passed into law PDD-63 on Critical Infrastructure Protection. The initiative designates nine physical and cyber-based systems essential to the minimum operations of the economy and government that are deemed vulnerable to possible terrorist attack—banking and finance; transportation; electricity, gas, and oil; telecommunications; emergency law enforcement; government services; emergency fire service; public health service; and the water supply. It should be noted that "Agriculture and Food Safety" is one of eight subgroups of the National Security Council's Weapons of Mass Destruction Preparedness Group, which was established in 1998 under Presidential Decision Directive 62 (PDD-62), "Combating Terrorism." The U.S. Department of Agriculture (USDA) chairs the Agriculture and Food Safety subgroup. However, as Henry Parker notes, the USDA is a relative latecomer to the national security and defense structure and presently lacks sufficient visibility and influence to champion greater federal attention to countering biological attacks against agriculture (which is, itself, invariably overshadowed by other terrorism-related issues). See Henry Parker, *Agricultural Bioterrorism: A Federal Strategy to Meet the Threat*, McNair Paper 65, Washington, D.C.: Institute for National Strategic Studies, National Defense University, March 2002, p. 30. For details on PDD-63, see The White House, *White Paper, The Clinton Administration's Policy on Critical Infrastructure Protection: Presidential Decision Directive 63*, Washington, D.C.: The White House, May 22, 1998.

[3] For example, Peter Chalk, "Terrorism, Infrastructure Protection, and the Agricultural Sector," testimony given before the Subcommittee on Oversight of Government Management, Restructuring and the District of Columbia, United States Senate, Washington, D.C., October 10, 2001.

tion, and factors that are contributing to the sector's risk of being exposed to deliberate disruption and sabotage.

Third, an agroterrorism[4] threat assessment was generated by equating inherent weaknesses within the agriculture sector to the capability requirements that would be necessary for the effective exploitation of the identified vulnerabilities. This matrix was then compared with known operational thresholds that have been established within the domain of human biowarfare.

Fourth, the costs and consequences of agricultural disasters were delineated by examining real-life incidents that have occurred in other parts of the world and by utilizing a taxonomy that measures "seriousness" of an incident in terms of its impact on overall public health, economic security, and political stability.

Finally, the principal findings from the primary fieldwork and secondary research were integrated and incorporated into the initial conceptual framework to generate a final report.

The general susceptibility of the agriculture and food industry to bioterrorism is difficult to address in a systematic manner due to the highly dispersed nature of the industry and because many of the risk evaluations used to assess vulnerability cannot be validated empirically. Nonetheless, the analysis contained in this report is useful to the extent that it highlights critical areas of weakness in the U.S. agricultural infrastructure and the potential ramifications of a concerted attack against the sector, which can be used to identify priority areas for future research. In addition, this study helps to enrich a body of work that, in comparison with literature on other areas of CIP, remains relatively thin and limited in its scope.[5]

---

[4] For the purposes of this report, *agroterrorism* is defined as the deliberate introduction of a disease agent, either against livestock or into the food chain, for purposes of undermining socioeconomic stability and/or generating fear. Depending on the disease agent and pathogenic vector chosen, agroterrorism is a tactic that can be used either to cause mass socioeconomic disruption or as a form of direct human aggression.

[5] Comprehensive analyses in the field of (deliberately orchestrated) biological threats to agriculture and the food chain are currently limited to the following published and unpublished works: Parker (2002); Paul Rogers, Simon Whitby, and Malcolm Dando, "Biological Warfare Against Crops," *Scientific American*, Vol. 280, No. 6, 1999; Norm Steele, *U.S. Agri-*

The Importance of the Agricultural Sector to the U.S. Economy

Agriculture and the food industry in general are extremely important to the social, economic, and, arguably, political stability of the United States. Although farming directly employs less than 3 percent of the American population, one in eight people works in an occupation that is directly supported by food production.[6] Cattle and dairy farmers alone earn between $50 billion and $54 billion a year through meat and milk sales,[7] while roughly $50 billion in revenues are generated every year through farm-related exports.

In 2001, food production constituted 9.7 percent of the U.S. gross domestic product (GDP), generating cash receipts in excess of $991 billion.[8] The share of agricultural commodities sold overseas is more than double the proportion of goods exported by other industries, an important and relevant factor in positively impacting Washington's balance of trade.[9] Added to these fiscal benefits is a solid

cultural Productivity, Concentration, and Vulnerability to Biological Weapons, unclassified defense intelligence assessment for the Department of Defense Futures Intelligence Program, Washington, D.C., January 14, 2000; Agricultural Research Service, *Econoterrorism, a.k.a. Agricultural Bioterrorism or Asymmetric Use of Biological Weapons,* unclassified briefing, Washington, D.C.: U.S. Department of Agriculture, February 28, 2000; Simon Whitby and Paul Rogers, "Anti-Crop Biological Warfare—Implications of the Iraqi and US Programs," *Defense Analysis,* Vol. 13, No. 3, 1997; Terry Wilson et al., "A Review of Agroterrorism, Biological Crimes and Biological Warfare Targeting Animal Agriculture," APHIS, Fort Detrick, Md., unpublished draft manuscript, 2001; John Gordon and Steen Bech-Nielsen, "Biological Terrorism: A Direct Threat to Our Livestock Industry," *Military Medicine,* Vol. 151, No. 7, 1986; and Agricultural Research Service, *Agriculture's Defense Against Biological Warfare and Other Outbreaks,* Washington, D.C.: USDA, December 1961.

[6] Agricultural Research Service, "Econoterrorism, a.k.a. Agricultural Bioterrorism or Asymmetric Use of Bioweapons," unclassified briefing before the United States Department of Agriculture, Washington, D.C., February 28, 2000. See also Parker (2002), p. 11.

[7] Overall livestock sales in 2001 were in excess of $108 billion. See "Agro-Terrorism Still a Credible Threat," *The Wall Street Journal,* December 26, 2001.

[8] Bureau of Economic Analysis, "Gross Domestic Product: First Quarter 2002 (Advance)," (available at http://www.bea.doc.gov/bea/newsrel/gdp102a.htm).

[9] Ellen Shell, "Could Mad Cow Disease Happen Here?" *The Atlantic Monthly,* Vol. 282, No. 3, 1998, p. 92; "Stockgrowers Warned of Terrorism Threat," *The Chieftain,* August 19, 1999.

foundation of agricultural research and development, which has helped to make U.S. farming the most efficient and productive in the world. Consequently, Americans spend less than 11 percent of their disposable income on food, compared with a global average of around 20 to 30 percent.[10]

Although they are significant, these figures represent only a fraction of the total value of agriculture to the U.S. economy. This is because the statistics do not take into account allied industries and services, such as suppliers, transporters, distributors, and restaurant chains.[11] The fiscal downstream effect of a major act of sabotage against the food industry would, in other words, be multidimensional, reverberating through other sectors of the U.S. economy and ultimately impacting directly on the American consumer.

Organization of This Report

The remainder of this report aims to expand the current debate on domestic homeland security by assessing the vulnerabilities of the agricultural and food industries to a deliberate act of biological terrorism. First, I outline the major vulnerabilities that exist in the agricultural sector and assess the capabilities that are needed to exploit those weaknesses. Next, I consider the likely outcomes of a successful agroterrorist attack and address the question of why terrorists have yet to employ agricultural assaults as a method of operation. I conclude the report with proposed recommendations for the U.S. policymaking community.

---

[10] Wilson et al. (2001), p. 22.

[11] Parker (2002), p. 11. According to the Department of Commerce, the economic multiplier effect of exported farm commodities alone is in the region of 20 to 1.

CHAPTER TWO

Vulnerability of U.S. Agriculture to Bio-Attacks

For a variety of reasons, the U.S. agricultural and food industry remains at risk to disruption and sabotage from deliberate bio-attacks. The sector's vulnerabilities principally stem from six factors:

- Concentrated and intensive contemporary farming practices in the United States
- Increased susceptibility of livestock to disease
- A general lack of farm/food-related security and surveillance
- An inefficient, passive disease-reporting system that is further hampered by a lack of trust between regulators and producers
- Veterinarian training that tends not to emphasize foreign animal diseases (FADs) or large-scale husbandry
- A prevailing focus on aggregate, rather than individual, livestock statistics.

Each of these factors is discussed in more detail in this chapter.

Concentrated and Intensive Contemporary Farming Practices

Agriculture is a large-scale and intensive business in the United States. Most dairies in the country can be expected to house at least 1,500 lactating cows at any one time, with some of the largest facilities containing upward of 10,000 animals.[1] These herds exist as highly crowded populations and tend to be bred and reared in extreme proximity to one another. The outbreak of a contagious disease at one of these facilities would be very difficult to contain, especially if the disease is airborne, and could necessitate the destruction of all exposed livestock—a formidable and very expensive task.[2] A case in point was the major outbreak of Exotic Newcastle Disease (END) in California in October 2002, which ultimately led to the slaughter of more than three million chickens in several counties across the state.[3]

Problems with contagious disease outbreaks are exacerbated by the distant and rapid dissemination of animals from farm to market (a pound of meat generally travels about 1,000 miles before it reaches the consumer's dinner table). A representative survey of U.S. barn auctions showed that between 20 and 30 percent of cattle were regularly consigned to non-slaughter destinations at least 30 miles from their original point of purchase and in many cases had crossed several states within 36 to 48 hours of leaving the sales yard.

Economic forces and the outsourcing of traditional agricultural activities have added considerably to the long-distance shipment of livestock in this country. In much of the dairy industry, for instance, there has been a trend toward contract calf-raising, which may in-

---

[1] See, for instance, Siobhan Gorman, "Bioterror Down on the Farm," *National Journal*, Vol. 27, July 1999, p. 812; and Agricultural Research Service, *Agriculture's Defense Against Biological Warfare and Other Outbreaks*, Washington, D.C.: USDA, 1961, p. 2. Currently, roughly three-quarters of all dairy commodities are concentrated in the hands of less than 10 percent of the country's cow and calf production facilities.

[2] The point at which eradication becomes unfeasible depends on current technical, economic, and political limits, but for most diseases, the critical number is generally considered to be around 1 percent of the susceptible population. In other words, once 1 percent of the population has been infected with an animal disease, eradication is no longer deemed to be advantageous. Obviously, "eradication-utility" calculations will vary according to the nature of the disease. For highly virulent pathogens, such as foot and mouth disease (FMD), a 1 percent threshold is unlikely to enter into the equation given the incredibly rapid dissemination of the virus and accepted rule that *all* infected and susceptible animals need to be eliminated.

[3] See "Exotic Newcastle Disease Update," California Department of Food and Agriculture, Animal Health Branch, press release, October 15, 2003. Affected counties included Imperial, Kern, Orange, Riverside, San Bernardino, San Diego, Santa Barbara, and Ventura.

volve operations that can number in excess of 30,000 animals from as many as 80 separate farms. With most operations, heifers are transported daily to rearing sites, and each week weaned calves are returned back to their original dairies.[4] The rapid transfer of livestock in this manner increases the risk that pathogenic agents will spread well beyond the locus of a specific outbreak before health officials become aware that a problem exists.

Increased Susceptibility of Livestock to Disease

U.S. livestock has become progressively more disease prone in recent years as a result of changes in husbandry practices and biotechnology innovations designed to increase the quality and quantity of meat production and to meet the specific requirements of individual vendors. Herds that have been subjected to such modifications—which have included everything from sterilization programs to dehorning, branding, and hormone injections—have typically suffered higher stress levels that have lowered the animals' natural tolerance to disease from contagious organisms and increased the viral and bacterial "volumes" that they normally shed in the event of an infection.[5]

Overuse and misuse of antibiotics to treat common ailments has exacerbated the problem by creating a pathogenic "natural selection" that has led to the emergence of increasingly powerful and resilient disease strains.[6] This process of microbial evolution has left livestock vulnerable to a whole new generation of virulent "super bugs" that

---

[4] Terry Wilson et al., "A Review Agroterrorism, Biological Crimes and Biological Warfare Targeting Animal Agriculture," unpublished draft manuscript, 2001, pp. 25–26.

[5] Comments by Paul Effler, Hawaii State epidemiologist, Transnational Security Threats in Asia conference, Honolulu, Hawaii, August 8–10, 2000.

[6] Overuse of antibiotics constitutes a critical trigger for microbial adaptation by forcing replication of plasmid in DNA and RNA codes, the dynamic of which causes mutation under stress. See Laurie Garrett, "The Return of Infectious Disease," *Foreign Affairs*, Vol. 75, No. 1, 1996, p. 67.

may be able to resist several families of antibiotics (or dozens of individual drugs) at any one time.[7]

Insufficient Farm/Food-Related Security and Surveillance

A deliberate act of sabotage is something the majority of the agricultural community has simply not thought about, much less physically sought to guard itself against. At the policy level, for example, it was not until October 1998 that the words "terrorism," "agriculture," and "biological weapons" were officially used in the same context by the U.S. Department of Agriculture (USDA) to assess potential vulnerabilities and threats to the agricultural industry.[8] U.S. farms, consequently, have tended to operate in a relatively open manner, seldom incorporating vigorous means to prevent unauthorized access or intrusion. The lack of secured barriers is especially true of outlying fields and feedlots and may also be the case with centralized facilities such as milking stands.

Security at animal auctions and barn sales also tends to be in short supply, with most of those operations devoid of organized on-site surveillance or monitoring. During the 1950s and 1960s, U.S. officials staged a number of test exercises at animal trade fairs to simulate the intentional dissemination of foot and mouth disease (FMD) and successfully introduced mock versions of the virus at several locations without their being intercepted. According to Terry Wilson, a senior USDA liaison officer stationed at Fort Detrick's Armed Forces Medical Intelligence Center in Maryland, little has changed over the

---

[7] See Parker, Henry, *Agricultural Bioterrorism: A Federal Strategy to Meet the Threat,* McNair Paper 65, Washington, D.C.: Institute for National Strategic Studies, National Defense University, March 2002, p. 13; Garrett (1996), p. 67; National Intelligence Council, *The Global Infectious Disease Threat and Its Implications for the United States,* National Intelligence Estimate 99-17D, Washington, D.C.: NIC, January 2000, p. 23; "Wonder Drugs at Risk," *The Washington Post,* April 19, 2001.

[8] Comments made by USDA officials during the National Research Council's National Security Implications of Advances in Biotechnology: Threats to Plants and Animals planning meeting, National Academy of Sciences, Washington, D.C., August 1999.

course of the intervening 40 or 50 years, and similar intrusions are just as possible today.[9]

Food processing and packing plants similarly tend to lack uniform security and safety preparedness measures, particularly the small- and medium-scale operations that have proliferated in recent years. Thousands of these facilities exist across the country, exhibiting uneven internal quality control standards, questionable biosurveillance practices, and highly transient, unscreened workforces.[10] Entry-exit controls are not always adequate (and occasionally do not exist at all), and even basic safety measures such as padlocking storage rooms may not be practiced. Moreover, many small-scale operations do not keep accurate records of their distribution network, meaning that it may not be possible to trace a tainted food item back to its original source of production.[11]

Inefficient Passive Disease-Reporting System

Responsibility for reporting unusual occurrences of livestock disease in the United States lies with the agricultural producers. However, in many cases, communication channels among state emergency management personnel are confusing and rudimentary and often lack guidelines that clearly designate the appropriate regulatory agencies and/or primary or secondary personnel that need to be contacted in the event of a serious viral or bacterial outbreak.

Equally important, farmers are often reluctant to immediately report contagious disease outbreaks, fearing that if they do so they will be forced to carry out uncompensated depopulation measures.

---

[9] Wilson et al. (2001), p. 26.

[10] During 2002, the Bush administration introduced plans to upgrade the screening of workers employed at food processing plants and packing facilities. It is not clear, however, how comprehensive those screening checks will be and to what extent they will apply to the thousands of small- and medium-scale plants that exist throughout the United States, which, due to the lack of federal inspectors, necessarily operate using a system of self-regulation.

[11] Author's interview with officials of the California Department of Health and Human Services, Sacramento, August 2000.

This unwillingness to quickly inform and engage the agricultural regulatory community reflects the fact that, at present, no standardized and consistent system exists to compensate producers affected by pathogenic outbreaks, with all indemnity payments currently determined on a case-by-case basis.[12] Moreover, even if large-scale culling of livestock is unlikely to take place, farmers may still not want to invite quarantine and disease management officials onto their premises due to the perceived message it could send to the surrounding community. Above all, they want to avoid giving the impression that a potential problem may exist, which could in turn lead to a loss of sales and jeopardize their domestic markets.[13]

The current operation of the U.S. animal disease-reporting system, in short, does little to promote early warning and identification of pathogenic outbreaks. This situation is troublesome because rapid confirmed diagnoses are vital to an effective emergency management system, particularly in the case of highly transmittable viral infections such as FMD.[14]

---

[12] The USDA is considering a review of indemnity provisions specifically related to FMD, which would authorize payments to cover both disinfection costs as well as the full market value of destroyed animals and related products and materials. For a detailed description of the proposed changes, see U.S. Department of Agriculture, *Foot and Mouth Disease Payment of Indemnity; Update of Provisions* (Docket Number 01-069-1), RIN 0597-AB34, November 2002.

[13] Author's interviews with agricultural specialists, University of California, Davis, Sacramento, August 2000.

[14] It should be noted that the catastrophic foot and mouth outbreak in the United Kingdom during 2001 has encouraged many farmers to be somewhat more proactive in disease reporting. According to David Huxoll, the former director of Emergency Programs at the Foreign Animal Disease Diagnostic Laboratory in Plum Island, New York, notifications of possible FMD cases quadrupled between September 2001 and mid-2002. Huxoll did not say, however, whether this vigilance has transcended to other viral and bacterial agents that are deemed to be threatening to agricultural livestock and trade (comments made during the Agricultural Publications Summit, Reno, Nevada, July 2002).

Inappropriate Veterinarian and Diagnostic Training

The pool of adequately trained veterinarians in the United States who are capable of recognizing and treating exotic livestock diseases is declining. In part, this situation reflects the smaller numbers of people entering the veterinary science field and pursuing large-scale husbandry studies specifically, which is itself a product of the lack of educational support and career financial incentives for livestock epidemiology and treatment.[15]

Just as important, this trend is indicative of the college curricula in many veterinary schools, which reportedly do not emphasize FADs, the focus instead being on diseases that are endemic to the United States.[16] The result has been a dearth of accredited state and local veterinarians who have either a background in farm animal diagnostics or the necessary expertise to deal with the most-threatening disease agents that are likely to be used in a deliberate act of agroterrorism.[17]

A Focus on Aggregate Rather Than Individual Livestock Statistics

The size and scale of contemporary agricultural enterprises in the United States, and the general movement toward larger herds and breeding operations, have largely precluded the option of farmers at-

---

[15] Comments made to author during the "AFBF Commodity Advisory Meeting," Capital Holiday Inn, Washington, D.C., January 2002. Most people who enter the veterinary science field tend to focus on domestic animals (such as dogs and cats) where the most money is to be made. Moreover, many families now purchase comprehensive pet insurance, which ensures that vet bills will be paid.

[16] Comments made by USDA officials attending the National Research Council National Security Implications of Advances in Biotechnology: Threats to Plants and Animals planning meeting, Washington, D.C., August 1999.

[17] Roughly 60,000 accredited veterinarians are currently registered on the Animal and Plant Health Inspection Service (APHIS) national database. See Animal and Plant Health Inspection Service, *National Veterinarian Accreditation Program (NVAP)*, Riverdale, Md., no date (available at http://www.aphis.usda.gov/vs/nvap/prt-txt_data.html as of October 2003).

tending to their animals on an individual basis. In most cases, producers are forced to monitor and regulate their livestock populations by referring to aggregate statistics, such as total milk yields.[18] This tendency, combined with the dwindling pool of accredited state and local livestock veterinarians (discussed above), has effectively resulted in more and more animals throughout the country receiving no form of comprehensive medical examination or remedial checkup. As a result, the possibility of emerging diseases being overlooked has become an increasingly real threat.

Capability Requirements for Carrying Out an Agroterrorist Attack

What makes the vulnerabilities inherent in the agriculture industry so worrying is that the capabilities for exploiting those weaknesses are not significant, and they are certainly less considerable than the operational requirements needed to carry out a human-directed bio-attack. Several factors account for this situation.

First, there is a large menu of agents from which to choose, with 15 "List A" pathogens identified by the Office International des Epizooties (OIE) as having the potential to severely affect agricultural populations and/or trade (see Table 2.1).[19]

---

[18] Comments made during a roundtable discussion on agroterrorism, University of California Davis, Sacramento, August 2000.

[19] The OIE defines List A diseases as those "that have the potential for very serious and rapid spread, irrespective of national borders, that are of serious socio-economic or public health consequence and that are of major importance in the international trade of animals and animal products." The OIE defines "List B" diseases as those "that are considered to be of socio-economic and/or public health importance within countries and that are significant in the international trade of animals and animal products." Included within this second category are:
- Multiple-species diseases (e.g., anthrax, aujeszky's disease, Q fever, rabies, screwworm)
- Sheep and goat diseases (e.g., Nairobi sheep disease, caprine brucellosis, contagious caprine pleuropneumonia, contagious agalactia)
- Cattle diseases (e.g., bovine brucellosis, bovine tuberculosis, malignant catarrhal fever, theileriosis)

Most of these diseases are environmentally hardy—being able to exist for extended periods of time on organic or inorganic matter—and tend not to be the focus of concerted livestock vaccination programs in the United States. Moreover, some of the most dangerous agents exist in regions close to American shores, are readily available from clinical specimens taken from dead or sick animals, and could be brought into the country with little risk of detection. A case in point is FMD (the agricultural equivalent to smallpox in terms of agent-agent spread), which is prevalent in South America, and which could easily be smuggled into the United States in manure stuck to the bottom of a shoe, for example, or via vesicular fluids absorbed onto a handkerchief.[20]

Second, many FADs cannot be transmitted to humans and therefore carry no risk of latent or accidental (human) infection. This quality precludes the necessity on the part of the perpetrator to have an advanced understanding of animal disease epidemiology and transmission modes, and eliminates the requirement for elaborate containment procedures, personal protective equipment (PPE), and/or prophylaxis antibiotics in the preparation of the agent.

- Equine diseases (e.g., equine influenza, glanders, equine infectious anaemia, epizootic lymphangitis)
- Swine diseases (e.g., porcine brucellosis, porcine reproductive and respiratory syndrome, transmissible gastroenteritis)
- Avian diseases (e.g., avian tuberculosis, avian chlamydiosis, marek's disease, fowl pox, fowl cholera)
- Bee diseases (e.g., European foulbrood, nosemosis of bees)
- Lagomorph diseases (e.g., rabbit haemorrhagic disease, myxomatosis)
- Fish diseases (e.g., spring viraemia of carp, infectious haematopoietic necrosis, viral haemorrhagic septicaemia)
- Mollusk diseases (e.g., MSX disease [*Haplosporidium nelsoni*], perkinsosis, bonamiosis)
- Crustacean diseases (e.g., white spot disease, yellowhead disease).

For further details, see the OIE classification of diseases (available at http://www.oie.int/eng/maladies/en_classification.htm).

[20] Comments made during the Agro-Terrorism: What Is the Threat? workshop, Cornell University, Ithaca, New York, November 2000.

Table 2.1
Animal Pathogens with Potential to Severely Impact Agricultural Populations

Pathogen	Mortality	Zoonotic
Foot and mouth disease virus	Less than 1% (however, morbidity is near 100%)	No
Classical swine fever (hog cholera)	High	No
African swine fever (ASF) virus	60%–100%, depending on isolate virulence	No
Rinderpest (RP) virus	High	No
Rift Valley fever (RVF) virus	10%–20% among adult populations; higher among young lambs, kids, and calves	Yes
Highly pathogenic avian influenza (AI) virus	Near 100%	Yes
Exotic Newcastle disease (END) virus	90%–100%	Yes
Peste des petits ruminants	50%–80%	No
Bluetongue (BT) virus	0%–50%	No
Sheep pox and goat pox (SGP) viruses	Near 50%, although can be as high as 95% in animals less than one month old	No
Swine vesicular disease (SVD)	Less than 1% (however, morbidity very high among pigs)	No
Vesicular stomatitis (VS) virus	Low (however, morbidity near 90%)	Yes
Lumpy skin disease (LSD) virus	Variable, depending on prevalence of insect vector	No
African horse sickness (AHS) virus	70%–95% (in horses); 10%–50% (in mules, according to species type)	No

SOURCE: Office International des Epizooties, n.d.

Third, if the objective of an agroterrorist act is human deaths, the food chain offers a low-tech mechanism that is nevertheless conducive to disseminating toxins and bacteria such as salmonella, *e-coli*, and botulinum (none of which requires any substantial scientific knowledge to isolate or develop). Developments in the farm-to-table food continuum have greatly increased the number of entry points for these agents, which combined with the lack of security and surveillance at many meat and vegetable processing and packing plants, have augmented the technical ease of orchestrating a food-borne attack. It is also worth bearing in mind that, at least at present, there are no definitive, real-time technologies that may be used to detect biological and chemical food contaminants, meaning that health authorities would know about an attack only *after* it has taken place.[21] Possibilities for preemptive action are therefore limited.

Fourth, animal diseases can spread quickly to affect large numbers of herds over a wide geographic area. This factor reflects both the intensive and concentrated modern farming practices in the United States and the increased susceptibility of livestock to viral and bacterial infections (discussed earlier in this chapter). Disease transmission models developed by the USDA, for example, have shown that a virus such as FMD can be expected to spread to as many as 25 states in as few as five days simply through the regulated movement of animals from farm to market.[22] If one takes into account that certain livestock consignments are unregulated (as either illegal shipments or re-selling or switching animals at market) and that in some cases the signs of clinical infection are not always immediately apparent (a pig afflicted with FMD, for instance, typically starts shedding vesicular droplets seven to ten days *prior* to symptoms becoming visibly evident), then the true rates of transmission could be even greater.

Finally, because agricultural livestock, itself, acts as the primary vector for pathogenic transmission, there is no weaponization obstacle to overcome. This particular "quality" of agroterrorism is important because the costs and technical difficulties associated with manufacturing disease agents for offensive purposes is frequently cited as one of the most significant barriers preventing nonstate offensive use of biological agents.[23]

---

[21] Comments made by USDA official during the Bioterrorism in the United States: Calibrating the Threat seminar, Carnegie Endowment for International Peace, Washington, D.C., January 2000.

[22] Author's interview with USDA officials, Washington, D.C., and Maryland, 1999–2000.

[23] A good summary of the technical constraints inherent in weaponizing biological agents can be found in Seth Carus, *Bioterrorism and Biocrimes: The Illicit Use of Biological Agents in the 20th Century,* Washington, D.C.: Center for Counterproliferation Research, National Defense University, 1999, pp. 26–29.

CHAPTER THREE

Potential Impact of a Major Act of Agroterrorism

Notwithstanding the relative operational ease of agricultural bio-assaults, there would be little point in investing the time and effort to carry out attacks against livestock and the food chain if the impact of such actions was not likely to be that great. The potential ramifications of terrorist actions are an important consideration in any vulnerability-risk assessment and, as such, have direct relevance to possible agroterror threat contingencies in the United States.

The effects of a concerted bio-assault on the U.S. food base would be far-reaching and could extend beyond the immediate agricultural community to affect other segments of society. It is possible to envision at least three major outcomes that could result from this particular manifestation of bioterrorism.

Economic Disruption

Perhaps among the most immediate effect of a major act of biological agroterrorism would be economic disruption, generating at least three expected levels of costs.

First, there would be the direct losses resulting from containment measures and the eradication of disease-ridden animals. The outbreak of a particularly severe case of FMD in Taiwan in 1997, for instance, immediately cost the Republic $10 million for vaccine purchases[1] and has since necessitated government spending in excess of

---

[1] Comments made during the Asia Pacific Center for Security Studies Senior Executive Course, Honolulu, Hawaii, April 22, 2002.

$4 billion for surveillance, cleaning and disinfection of affected live-stock premises, and related viral eradication programs.[2] A 1994 USDA study similarly concluded that if a disease such as African swine fever (ASF) were to ever become entrenched in the United States, the direct financial impact over a ten-year period would be at least $5.4 billion (which equates to roughly 2 percent of the agricultural sector's total annual revenues).[3] One observer estimated that the true cost of such an outbreak in today's dollars could be as much as three to five times higher than that.[4]

Second, indirect multiplier effects would accrue from both the compensation paid to farmers for the destruction of agricultural commodities[5] and the revenue deficits suffered by both directly and indirectly related industries. As the 2001 outbreak of FMD in the United Kingdom illustrated, the extent of these costs can be very high. By the end of that year, well over $1.6 billion (U.S. dollars) had been paid in compensation to farmers affected by mass culling operations. Losses to tourism as a result of trip cancellations following the quarantine of farms located in or near popular travel destinations (such as England's Lake District) were just as serious and estimated to have been in the range of $4 billion (U.S. dollars, at an exchange rate of US$1 to 0.60 pence).[6]

Third, international trade costs would be incurred in the form of protective embargoes imposed by major external export partners.

---

[2] Terry Wilson et al., "A Review of Agroterrorism, Biological Crimes and Biological Warfare Targeting Animal Agriculture," unpublished draft manuscript, 2001, p. 24; Henry Parker, *Agricultural Bioterrorism: A Federal Strategy to Meet the Threat,* McNair Paper 65, Washington, D.C.: Institute for National Strategic Studies, National Defense University, March 2002, p. 15.

[3] See C. Renlemann and C. Spinelli, "An Economic Assessment of the Costs and Benefits of African Swine Fever Prevention," *Animal Health Insight,* Spring/Summer 1994.

[4] Parker (2002), p. 15.

[5] Although the United States has no standardized system of compensation in place, federal funds would be forthcoming in the event of a large-scale agricultural disaster, such as a multi-focal outbreak of FMD.

[6] "Farmers Paid GBP1 Bn for Culled Animals," *The Daily Telegraph,* June 30, 2001; "After Foot and Mouth," *The Economist,* May 5, 2001; "Spring Returns to Rural Britain, But Not Tourists," *The Washington Post,* March 16, 2001.

One study from California,[7] which presented eight different scenarios associated with a theoretical FMD outbreak, concluded that each day of delay in instituting effective eradication and control measures would cost the state $1 billion in trade sanctions. These projected financial burdens could be even greater when one considers the legalities of the United States' current export treaties, which allow overseas trading partners to automatically institute wholesale export bans in the event of either minor or major FAD occurrences. In effect, this means that even small-scale, or indeed isolated, disease outbreaks (both of which are easier to perpetrate than more-widespread pandemics) have the capacity to generate costly, and possibly lingering, effects on trade. In this sense, agroterrorism has significant utility in terms of a low-cost (to the perpetrator) to high-yield (vis-à-vis economic effects on agriculture) ratio.

Cost considerations regarding international trade are equally as pertinent to deliberate product contamination. Perhaps the best example of this was the Chilean grape scare of 1989. This incident involved a plot by anti-Pinochet extremists to lace fruit bound for the United States with sodium cyanide. Although only a handful of grapes was actually contaminated, import suspensions subsequently imposed by the United States, Canada, Denmark, Germany, and Hong Kong cost Chile in excess of $200 million (U.S. dollars) in lost revenue earnings.[8]

---

[7] Author's interview with California Department of Food and Agriculture (CDFA) officials, Sacramento, September 2000. See also "Eastern Oregon Farmers Ready to Eradicate Cattle Disease Threat," *The Oregonian*, August 17, 1999.

[8] See Ron Purver, *Chemical and Biological Terrorism: A New Threat to Public Safety*, Conflict Studies No. 295, London, UK: Research Institute for the Study of Conflict and Terrorism, 1996/1997, pp. 13–14; David Rapoport, "Terrorists and Weapons of the Apocalypse," paper presented before the Future Developments in Terrorism conference, Cork, Ireland, March 1999, pp. 13–14; and "Plant Scientists Sound the Alarm on Agroterrorism," *The Philadelphia Inquirer*, September 13, 1999.

Loss of Political Support and Confidence in the Government

A successful bio-attack against the U.S. agricultural sector could undermine the public's confidence in and support of the government. For example, a successful release of contagious agents against livestock could cause the public to question the safety of the food supply and possibly lead individuals to speculate over the effectiveness of existing contingency planning against weapons of mass destruction in general. Critics, perhaps unfairly, may demand to know in hindsight why the country's intelligence services failed to detect that an attack was imminent and why the agricultural sector was left exposed. Graphic images of diseased cows and sheep would likely appear in the media, serving to demonstrate the extreme susceptibility of animals to disease and the vulnerability of all animal life, including humans, to deadly pathogens. The combined effect of these factors could potentially initiate a chain reaction of sociopolitical events, which, if not carefully controlled, act to undermine the public's trust in both state and federal governance.

The mechanics of dealing with an act of agricultural bioterrorism could also generate public criticism. Containing a major disease outbreak would necessitate the slaughter of hundreds of thousands of animals, particularly for cases in which no concerted vaccination program is in place. The 1999 nipah virus epidemic in Malaysia, for instance, resulted in more than 800,000 pigs being shot dead, while the 2001 FMD outbreak in the UK had by the end of June of that year (at the height of the epidemic) resulted in nearly 3.5 million animals being destroyed (see Table 3.1).[9]

Euthanizing animals in such numbers has the potential to generate vigorous opposition from the general population, not to mention farmers and animal rights advocates, particularly if the slaughtering involved susceptible but non-symptomatic herds (in so-called *fire breaker* operations) and/or wildlife. To be sure, mass eradication of

---

[9] "Pig-Borne Epidemic Kills 117," *The Sydney Morning Herald,* April 10, 1999; "Farmers Paid GBP1 Bn for Culled Animals," 2001.

Table 3.1
Culling Operations During the UK FMD Outbreak, February–June 2001

Total FMD Cases to June 28	1,799
Animals slaughtered	3,347,000
Animals awaiting slaughter	11,000
Carcasses awaiting disposal	9,000
Total number of affected premises	8,450

SOURCE: "Farmers Paid GBP1 Bn for Culled Animals," *Daily Telegraph,* June 30, 2001.

livestock has occurred in the United States without triggering widespread civil disquiet. However, such operations have not involved large-scale animal husbandry (for the most part they have focused on poultry flocks), nor have they been the subject of intensive media interest and scrutiny. The limited news and television coverage to date of U.S. eradication of livestock has particular relevance in assessing the possible fallout from culling measures, because the American public has yet to see firsthand the effects of mass animal depopulation and may be somewhat unprepared for such images.[10]

The potential political ramifications of mass animal eradication involving large-scale husbandry is well exemplified by the UK FMD outbreak. The measures instituted by the Blair government to stem the epidemic elicited significant opposition from farmers, scientists, politicians (many of whom claimed the government overreacted to the situation), and the public, significantly undermining the domestic support base of a Labour administration that hitherto had been relatively popular.[11] The following commentary by Simon Jenkins in *The Times* newspaper is representative of the extreme criticism that was directed at the Blair government during the crisis:

> Policy on foot and mouth disease (FMD) is now running on autopilot . . . Nothing in the entire history of the common agriculture policy has been so crazy. The slaughter is not declining but running at 80,000 a day . . . At the last estimate, 95 percent of the three to four million animals dead or awaiting death are

[10] Author's telephone interview, Agriculture Research Service official, October 2003.

[11] Author's personal observations while in the United Kingdom, June–July 2001.

healthy . . . The obscenity of the policy is said to be irrelevant "because of its success." Yet what other industry would be allowed to protect its profits by paying soldiers with spades to kill piglets and drown lambs in streams? What other industry could get civil servants to bury cattle alive or take potshots at cows from a 60ft range? What other industry can summon teams from Whitehall to roam the lanes of the Forest Dean, as one frantic farmer telephoned me, "like Nazi stormtroopers seeking healthy sheep to kill on the authority of a map reference"? [The government] is killing healthy animals not from any concern of welfare but to help livestock exports. I cannot imagine another industry that would be protected in this appalling fashion.[12]

Even if large-scale culling operations are seen as being acceptable, the removal of diseased carcasses could be just as challenging in terms of gaining public support. The quickest and easiest way to dispose of destroyed livestock is either by burying the bodies in landfills covered with quicklime or by incinerating them in pits lined with straw, railroad ties, and coal. However, utilizing such methods in an ecologically "friendly" manner is feasible only if a small number of animals are involved. Incinerating thousands of carcasses over burning material, for instance, would create a huge, smoldering, open blaze as well as a very visible atmospheric pollution problem, both of which would attract widespread criticism. Mass burial is likely to be just as contentious, not least because of the risk it may pose to ground-water supplies and the possibility that it could render large areas of land essentially unusable for many years (of particular concern in heavily urbanized states). On the other hand, the longer that officials leave diseased carcasses out in the open, the higher the prob-

---

[12] "This Wretched Cult of Blood and Money," *The Times,* May 23, 2001. It should be noted that this quote reflects a fair degree of journalistic license, and there is no evidence to suggest that eradication of the sort that is suggested actually occurred. Nonetheless, the article is indicative of the very negative public reception that government-instituted mass depopulation measures received at the height of the FMD outbreak.

ability that the bodies will decay and become the source of another epidemic spread—an equally unacceptable outcome.[13]

Social Instability

Beyond the immediate economic and political impact, bioterrorist assaults against agriculture could potentially elicit fear and anxiety among the public and possibly trigger socially disruptive rural-urban migrations. Several animal pathogens are *zoonotic*, meaning they have the ability to "jump" species and affect humans as well as livestock. Examples of these microbial agents include avian influenza (AI), Rift Valley fever (RVF), vesicular stomatitis (VS), and screwworm. Should an epidemic of any one of these diseases occur in the United States, it could have severe repercussions by setting off a nationwide health scare, particularly if human deaths were to occur. Terrorists could use this state of public anxiety to their advantage to create a general atmosphere of fear without having to actually carry out indiscriminate civilian-oriented attacks that could both incur mass reprisals and alienate actual and/or potential support.

Two pathogenic outbreaks that occurred in 1999 illustrate how rapidly such events can occur and the extent to which zoonotic dis-

---

[13] Corrie Brown, "Impact and Risk of Foreign and Animal Diseases," *Vet Med Today,* Vol. 208, No. 7, p. 1039. See also John Gordon and Steen Bech-Nielsen, "Biological Terrorism: A Direct Threat to Our Livestock Industry," *Military Medicine,* Vol. 151, No. 7, 1986, p. 360. The USDA has attempted to come to grips with the problem of mass carcass disposal by considering animal rendering as a possible way to deal with livestock slaughtered from quarantined farms. To test the viability of this alternative, in 1998 the USDA computer-simulated an outbreak of FMD in which (hypothetically) destroyed animals were exposed to extreme heat, reduced, and reprocessed into feed meal as part of the emergency containment process. However, within one week, the test system had been completely overwhelmed and could no longer deal with the volume of animal protein it was receiving. Following the exercise, officials with the USDA's Animal and Plant Health Inspection Service (APHIS) concluded that rendering was ineffectual in dealing with mass carcass disposal, and in the event of a major disease outbreak, the only realistic way of quickly disposing of animal corpses would be to burn or bury them. USDA officials have since conceded that gaining public and political acceptance of these methods, or developing viable alternatives to them, remains one of the most challenging problems currently facing the USDA in contingency planning for future emergencies.

eases can impact the lives of ordinary citizens. The first case involved the spread of the Malaysian nipah virus, which, in addition to devastating the swine population of the Negri Sembilan province, claimed the lives of 117 villagers. The most serious part of the outbreak, which lasted just over a month, caused thousands of people to desert their homes and abandon their livelihoods. Many of these individuals fled as "environmental refugees," swelling already crowded shanty towns on the outskirts of Kuala Lumpur.[14] The second case occurred in New York City and involved an outbreak of West Nile Virus (WNV), which apparently was brought into the country by migrating birds from Africa and the Middle East. The disease, which was previously unknown to the United States, quickly spread to humans, several of whom died as a result of massive heart and liver failure. A serious public health scare ensued, which was heightened by the epidemiological difficulty (at least initially) in definitively determining the pathogen's type, source, and transmission mode.[15]

A food-borne agroterrorist attack could do equally as well as a zoonotic pathogenic outbreak in terms of eliciting public panic and creating general social instability. Because most processed food is disseminated to catchment areas within a matter of hours, a single case of chemical or biological adulteration could have significant latent ongoing effects, especially if the source of the contamination was not immediately apparent and acute or chronic ailments resulted.

---

[14] "Malay Troops Slaughter Pigs in War on Virus," cnn.com International Web site, March 20, 1999; "Pig-Borne Epidemic Kills 117," 1999.

[15] Comments made during a special panel on WNV during the International Conference on Emerging Infectious Diseases, Atlanta, Georgia, July 2000. A second WNV outbreak in 2002, which affected Louisiana and Illinois in particular (in terms of both relative morbidity and mortality), has certainly done nothing to mitigate U.S. public health concerns surrounding the disease.

Agroterrorism to Generate Financial Capital and as a Form of Blackmail

The low probability of detecting an intentional biological assault against agriculture potentially makes it a useful modus operandi for terrorists (and other criminals in general) for raising funds. One conceivable way of generating working capital through agroterrorist attacks would be to create and then exploit fluctuations in the commodity futures market. An attack that severely cripples the U.S. cattle industry, for instance, would probably result in heightened demand, and associated price increases, for the products of America's major beef and dairy competitors.[16] An astute perpetrator could take advantage of these market dynamics by investing in certain stocks before carrying out the assault, allowing the "natural" economic laws of supply and demand to take effect, and then garnering increased dividend premiums.[17]

In addition, the mechanics and potential impact of agroterrorism give this type of aggression a sizable payoff in the form of extortion and blackmail. Unlike with human-directed biological threats, terrorists could firmly establish the credibility of their intention to carry out a bio-assault by proceeding with an attack, safe in the knowledge that they are unlikely to elicit massive retaliation from a government that feels all limits on coercive counteraction have been lifted. Certainly, destroying cattle en masse would not elicit the same sort of institutional counterterrorist response as would killing thousands of civilians with the plague or anthrax. Moreover, given the potential immediate and latent damage that could be inflicted by repeated attacks, both state and federal governments would have a strong incentive to negotiate with the terrorists.

---

[16] This statement is not axiomatic. Following the "Mad Cow" crisis in the United Kingdom during the 1990s, for example, the British temporarily shunned all beef products, irrespective of their place of origin.

[17] Personal correspondence between author and USDA officials, Washington, D.C., July 1999. See also "Administration Plans to Use Plum Island to Combat Terrorism," *The New York Times*, September 21, 1999.

Biological Assaults Against Agriculture and Terrorists' Modus Operandi

Despite the ease with which an act of agroterrorism could be carried out and the serious impact of a successful assault (especially the economic and political fallout), it is unlikely to constitute a primary form of terrorist aggression. Indeed, agroterrorism would probably be viewed as being too "mundane" in comparison with traditional terrorist tactics (which focus on more-spectacular, human-directed atrocities) because it does not produce immediate, visible effects. The impact of bio-assaults on livestock and the food chain, although significant, is delayed and lacks a single focal point for media attention. More specifically, there is no drama of the sort that results from a suicide bombing or a September 11–style attack, which is absolutely essential to creating the hostility and panic that such acts are designed to elicit.[18]

In this light, it is perhaps understandable why biological attacks against agriculture have not been more of a problem. In fact, since 1912 there have been only 12 documented cases involving the substate use of pathogenic agents to infect livestock or contaminate food produce. Of those 12 incidents, only two could in any way be termed terrorist in nature: the 1984 Rajneeshee salmonella food poisoning in Oregon and the 1952 Mau Mau plant toxin incident in Kenya (see Table 3.2).

That being said, attacks against agriculture could emerge as a favored form of secondary aggression designed to contribute to the social upheaval caused by more-traditional terrorist tactics, such as random bombings. The ability to employ cheap and unsophisticated means to undermine a government's economic base, and possibly overwhelm its public-management resources, give livestock and food-related attacks an attractive cost/benefit payoff for any group seeking

---

[18] See, for instance, Brian Jenkins, "Future Trends in International Terrorism," in Robert Slater and Michael Stohl (eds.), *Current Perspectives on International Terrorism,* London, UK: Macmillan Press, 1988.

Table 3.2
Selected 20th-Century Agriculture and Food Bioterrorism Incidents

Year	Nature of Incident	Alleged Perpetrators
	Confirmed Use of an Agent	
1997	The spread of hemorrhagic virus among the wild rabbit population in New Zealand	New Zealand farmers
1996	Food poisoning using shigella in a Texas hospital	Hospital lab worker
1995	Food poisoning of estranged husband using ricin	Kansas physician
1984	Food poisonings using salmonella in salad bars in Oregon restaurants	Rajneeshee Cult
1970	Food poisoning of Canadian college students	Estranged roommate
1964	Food poisoning in Japan using salmonella and dysentery agents	Japanese physician
1952	Use of African bush milk to kill livestock	Mau Mau (an insurgent organization in Kenya)
1939	Food poisoning in Japan using salmonella	Japanese physician
1936	Food poisoning in Japan using salmonella	Japanese physician
1916	Food poisoning in New York using various biological agents	Dentist
1913	Food poisoning in Germany using cholera and typhus	Former chemist employee
1912	Food poisoning in France using salmonella and toxic mushrooms	French druggist
	Threatened Use of an Agent	
1984	Attempt to kill a racehorse with pathogens (insurance scam); confirmed possession	Two Canadians
1984	Threat to introduce FMD into wild pigs, which would then infect livestock; no confirmed possession	Australian prison inmate

SOURCE: Carus (1999); Parker (2002), pp. 2–21.

to overcome power differences between itself and the sovereign state it is targeting. These considerations have particular relevance to an organization such as al-Qaeda, which has repeatedly stated its intention to conduct economic warfare against the United States (Osama bin Laden regards Washington's wealth as the main anchor of a morally bankrupt and dysfunctional Western system that he seeks to overthrow), and which has explicitly endorsed the acquisition and use of biological agents to undermine U.S. interests (in whatever manner possible) as a religious duty for all "true" Muslims.[19]

It is also worth noting that the potential viability of employing livestock diseases as a form of indirect warfare has long been recognized, at least at the nation-state level. As far back as World War II, the British were experimenting with "cattle cakes"—cow "snacks" laced with anthrax—as a way of crippling the German beef industry.[20] Before terminating its biological weapons (BW) program in 1969, the United States had field-tested both hog cholera and END for offensive purposes.[21] A key component of Soviet BW efforts was similarly directed toward the development of agricultural pathogens, including FMD, rinderpest, and sheep/goat pox viruses.[22] During the apartheid years, the Republic of South Africa weaponized both FMD and ASF for use in Angola, Namibia (then Southwest Africa), and

---

[19] "The World's Newest Fear: Germ Warfare," *The Vancouver Sun,* September 24, 2001; "Fear and Breathing," *The Economist,* September 29, 2001.

[20] Siobhan Gorman, "Bioterror Down on the Farm," *National Journal,* Vol. 27, p. 813. According to Seth Carus (*Bioterrorism and Biocrimes: The Illicit Use of Biological Agents in the 20th Century,* Washington, D.C.: Center for Counterproliferation Research, National Defense University, 1999, p. 87–88), the German Secret Service was experimenting with anti-livestock biological agents even earlier than World War II. Carus attests that various programs involving glanders and anthrax cultures were developed during World War I as part of a concerted effort to destroy animals that were deemed to be contributing to the Allied war effort in Europe. Targets included sheep, cattle, horses, mules, and donkeys, and other ruminants in Russia, Romania, Argentina, and the United States.

[21] Wilson et al. (2001), p. 10. See also E. Regis, *The Biology of Doom: The History of America's Secret Germ Warfare Project,* New York: Henry Holt and Company, 1999; and L. Cole, *The Eleventh Plague: The Politics of Biological and Chemical Warfare,* New York: W.H. Freeman and Company, 1997. On 12 occasions between 1964 and 1967, Fidel Castro accused the United States of using animal, plant, and human viruses and insects to harm and disrupt the Cuban economy. He also later claimed that livestock pathogens were intentionally introduced into Cuba at least six times following the formal termination of Washington's BW program, once in 1971 and in 1979 and twice in 1981 and in 1985.

[22] Wilson et al. (2001), pp. 13–14.

Zimbabwe. It is now also known that at least two anti-animal agents—FMD and camelpox (although in the latter case, it may have been a surrogate for smallpox)—had been developed in Iraq prior to the 1991 Gulf War.[23]

There are several ways in which a deliberate act of agricultural sabotage or terrorism could occur on U.S. soil, using a variety of different causative agents and dissemination methods. However, attacks directed against the cattle, swine, or poultry industries or that are instituted via the food chain pose the most serious danger for latent ongoing effects and general socioeconomic and political disruption. Possible threat scenarios could include:

- *The introduction of a zoonotic pathogen designed to kill both humans and animals.* One such possible agent is screwworm myiasis. The parasite is endemic throughout the world, and it is a serious concern in areas close to American shores. Screwworm myiasis is caused by the Cochliomyia hominivorax maggot, which feeds on the living tissue of any warm-blooded mammal. Cattle are easily infected with the agent because the female maggot is able to oviposit eggs (in excess of 400 in a single laying) in a wide range of wounds common to these animals, including tick bites and cuts or lesions resulting from dehorning and castration. An initial infestation has the potential to quickly spread to urban areas (adult flies can travel up to 200 miles on wind currents) where it would pose an immediate health risk to both domestic pets and humans.[24]
- *The introduction of a non-zoonotic pathogen designed to undermine the public's support of and confidence in the government and trigger mass economic destabilization.* The most viable agent in this case is FMD, which is easy to acquire, environmentally hardy, and highly contagious. The means for disseminating FMD could be

---

[23] Comments made during the National Security Implications of Advances in Biotechnology: Threats to Plants and Animals Steering Group meeting, National Academy of Sciences, Washington, D.C., August 1999. See also Wilson et al. (2001), pp. 11–12 and 14.

[24] Author's interview with CDFA officials, Sacramento, California, August 14, 2000.

as simple as scraping a viral sample directly onto a cow grazing in a remote field or merely introducing the agent into a silage bin or feedlot at an auction barn. Because the disease is highly contagious, and because contemporary U.S. farming practices are concentrated and intensive, a multifocal outbreak across several states would be virtually assured.[25]

- *An attack carried out further down the food chain, either for blackmail purposes or as a form of direct aggression against humans.* Packing plants that deal with fresh fruits and vegetables and small-scale food manufacturers, particularly those specializing in ready-to-eat meats or aggregated foodstuffs, have the greatest threat of attack. These facilities are especially vulnerable because in general they do not practice uniform biosecurity methods, they do not use heat in food processing (a good "front-end" barrier against pathogenic contamination), and they deal in already-prepared produce that does not require cooking (a good "back-end" defense against microbial introduction). Likely agents in this case include bacteria and toxins such as salmonella (which can be grown in a household kitchen), e. coli 0157 (which is commonly shed by cattle), and botulinum (which has no odor, does not visibly spoil food, and does not require sophisticated equipment to manufacture).[26]

---

[25] Comments made during the Agro-Terrorism: What Is the Threat? workshop, Cornell University, Ithaca, New York, November 12–13, 2000.

[26] Comments made during the Bioterrorism in the United States: Calibrating the Threat seminar, Carnegie Endowment for International Peace, Washington, D.C., January 2000.

CHAPTER FOUR

Policy Recommendations

The United States, more by luck than by design, has not experienced the type of major agricultural and other food-related disasters to which other countries and polities, such as the United Kingdom, Malaysia, and Taiwan, have been subjected in recent times. As a result, there has been no real appreciation of either the consequences or the potential threat of such events taking place in this country.

This false sense of security has been further fueled by the agricultural sector's relative "invisibility" in American society.[1] This situation is reflected in the structure of the U.S. agricultural emergency preparedness-and-response system, which has yet to be given the resources it needs to develop into a truly integrated and comprehensive system capable of addressing mass multifocal contingencies. In fact, in fiscal year 2000 (FY00), the U.S. Congress rejected an Animal and Plant Health Inspection Service (APHIS) request for $139 million to enhance the country's overall disease-management capabilities, and in FY01 only $500,000 was federally appropriated to support specific

---

[1] Three main factors account for the "invisibility" of the agricultural sector in the United States. First, most Americans take it for granted that food is readily available and that their food is safe, and would find it difficult to conceive of a situation in which food would be scarce, expensive, or risky to consume. Second, modern agricultural practices in the United States, which are increasingly concentrated, have led to a dramatic reduction in the number of individual farms in the country (2.2 million in 1998 compared with 6.3 million in 1929). Third, technological innovation has resulted in fewer Americans being directly employed in agricultural production: farming accounted for 2.6 percent of the U.S. workforce in 1998, down from 23 percent in 1929 (Henry Parker, *Agricultural Bioterrorism: A Federal Strategy to Meet the Threat*, McNair Paper 65, Washington, D.C.: Institute for National Strategic Studies, National Defense University, March 2002, p. 29). See also U.S. Department of Agriculture, *Agriculture—Farms, Acreage, and Foreign Trade: 1990–1998*, Washington, D.C.: National Agricultural Statistics Service, No. 1441, 1999.

counterterrorism research in the USDA, an amount representing just 0.003 percent of the total homeland security budget ($16 billion) allocated for that year.[2]

Just as important, biosecurity and surveillance at many of the country's food processing and rendering plants generally remain inadequate. Formal state and federal inspections of these sites are rudimentary, and current oversight of food production is inconsistent. In discussing this situation during a 2001 U.S. Senate hearing in Washington, D.C., Robert Robinson, managing director of Natural Resources and the Environment at the U.S. General Accounting Office (GAO), observed, "If you are producing a packaged open-faced meat or poultry sandwich, you get inspected daily. . . . If, on the other hand, you are producing a close-faced sandwich with identical ingredients, you get inspected . . . on average once every five years."[3]

In specific terms, the following key deficiencies in the current U.S. agricultural emergency-management system can be identified:

- A lack of resources, particularly those for quickly identifying, containing, and eradicating large-scale disease outbreaks
- Insufficient personnel with appropriate training in recognition and treatment of FADs

---

[2] Author's interview with APHIS officials, Maryland, September 1999; Parker (2002), p. 30; U.S. Department of Agriculture, *Advisory Committee on Agricultural Biotechnology,* Federal Register Notice 64, Washington, D.C., n.d.

[3] Testimony of Robert Robinson, "Food Safety and Security," given before the Subcommittee on Oversight of Government Management, Restructuring, and the District of Columbia of the Committee on Governmental Affairs, U.S. Senate, October 10, 2001. Some significant food contamination scares have already occurred in the United States. In 1996, for instance, an unknown caller notified Wisconsin police authorities that animal feed and liquid fat intended for dairy farms in Minnesota, Michigan, and Illinois had been laced with chlordane, an environmentally stable pesticide. Although no cows were ever actually infected, the scare resulted in the destruction of 4,000 tons of animal feed and 500,000 pounds of liquid fat at a cost of $4 million. An earlier case in Wisconsin involved the contamination of silage with an organophosphate insecticide for corn root worm, resulting in the death of more than 130 beef cattle in 24 hours. No one was ever apprehended in connection with the poisoning, although authorities believe an individual with a grudge against the targeted farmer may have been responsible (Nicholas Neher, "Food Terrorism: The Need for a Coordinated Response—the Wisconsin Experience," unpublished position paper prepared for the USDA's Agricultural Resource Management Division, n.d., pp. 6–7).

- An overall decline in the pool of diagnosticians, which is a result of insufficient educational support for the study of veterinary science
- Inadequate forensic coordination among the agricultural, intelligence, and domestic criminal justice communities
- An emergency response program that is limited by an unreliable passive disease-reporting system and which is further hampered by a lack of communication and trust between regulators and producers
- Inconsistent food surveillance and inspections at processing and packing plants.

The catastrophic events of September 11 have, to a certain extent, focused greater national attention on some of these weaknesses and the general vulnerability of the U.S. agricultural sector to deliberate sabotage and disruption. The Agriculture Research Service's (ARS's) counterterrorism budget for FY03, for instance, has been increased to $5.5 million (from a FY02 base that had remained unchanged at $500,000). This amount is in addition to the $328 million in Emergency Supplementary Assistance (ESA) that the USDA as a whole has received to augment overall preparedness and consequence management efforts related to intentional attacks against the country's food supply.[4] More important is the extra funding that has been made available to APHIS—the USDA's main frontline "combat unit" when it comes to rapid disease response, containment, and control—which, in FY03, will amount to $146 million.[5]

---

[4] Author's interview with USDA officials, Washington, D.C., May 23, 2002. See also United States Department of Agriculture, *Budget Summary 2003* (available at http://www.usda.gov/agency/obpa/Budget-Summary/2003).

[5] "Agriculture Budget Proposes Increases in Key Areas," USDA news release, No. 0031.02, February 4, 2002; U.S. Department of Agriculture, *Budget Summary 2003.* Key areas for this funding include:
- Plant and animal health monitoring ($48 million)
- Overseas disease monitoring ($5 million)
- Border inspections ($19 million)
- Food safety inspections ($28 million)
- Research ($34 million)

However, federal fiscal resources that are available to the USDA for agroterrorism purposes remain marginal—amounting to only a fraction of the more than $4 billion that has been earmarked for general (i.e., human and nonhuman) anti-bioterrorism purposes over the next two years[6]—and no provision has been made in the ESA to support in-depth state and local first response (a main area of weakness in terms of national contingency efforts).[7] Moreover, agriculture has yet to be officially recognized as a critical infrastructural node for the purposes of PDD-63 (although it is included as part of President Bush's national post–September 11 counterterrorist strategy) and was conspicuously absent in a GAO report on combating terrorism released nine days after the attacks on the World Trade Center and Pentagon.[8]

The United States ignores the continuing vulnerability of the agricultural sector at its own peril. Measures can, and indeed should, be instituted to pursue a more aggressive and coordinated strategy to securing the industry from deliberate attack, an approach that would have the ancillary benefit of augmenting general prevention and response efforts against naturally occurring disease outbreaks in food and livestock. These initiatives should build on programs already under way; leverage existing federal, state, and local capabilities; and involve key customers, stakeholders, and partners.[9] At least six policy recommendations can be made for the short and medium term:

- Diagnostic, management, response, and other scientific and technical services ($12 million).

[6] "House Passes $4.6 Billion Bioterror Bill," *The Associated Press,* May 22, 2002.

[7] ESA funding is earmarked for the following areas only:
- Improving agricultural quarantine inspection and emergency management systems within the USDA's Animal and Plant Health Inspection Service
- Accelerating construction of facilities to support ARS animal health research and APHIS diagnostic and vaccine programs
- Upgrading laboratory se`curity and improving operational security equipment.

[8] Parker (2002), p. 1, 30. The GAO specifically excluded consideration of the agricultural sector in its analysis because it was not included as one of the critical systems specified under PDD-63.

[9] Parker (2002) p. 31.

First, a comprehensive needs analysis should be undertaken to ascertain appropriate investment requirements for the federal emergency management infrastructure, particularly in relation to:

- Continuing foreign animal disease intramural research in ARS laboratories
- Regular preparedness and response exercises and programs, utilizing both in-house simulated tabletop and "day-after" games as well as full-scale field simulations
- The upgrading of existing diagnostic laboratories to biosafety level 4 (BSL4) (necessary for high-level research on the most-contagious and dangerous animal pathogens)[10]
- Integrated electronic field diagnostic and communication systems and emergency control centers that can take advantage of the very latest information and data management technology.

Second, steps need to be taken to increase the number of state and local personnel who have the requisite skills to identify and treat exotic animal diseases. Some initial reform of the nationwide veterinary science curriculum, with a greater emphasis on developing and supporting ongoing FAD and large-scale husbandry education components, would be useful in this regard. A review of the training and certification requirements of non-veterinarian professionals (such as ranch handlers) who examine the condition of individual animals on a regular basis would also be helpful. Together with appropriately accredited local and state veterinarians, these individuals would help to fulfill an important USDA "force multiplier" function by providing

---

[10] The USDA currently relies on two main centers for research and information on virulent and contagious animal viruses: the Foreign Animal Disease Diagnostic Laboratory on Plum Island, New York, and the National Veterinary Services Laboratories in Ames, Iowa. However, neither facility has been certified above BSL 3, meaning that they cannot conduct concerted research into the most dangerous livestock pathogenic agents; currently, the USDA relies on the Centers for Disease Control in Atlanta and the U.S. Army Medical Research Institute for Infectious Diseases at Fort Detrick for these assessments (from comments made during the Agro-Terrorism: What Is the Threat? workshop, Cornell University, Ithaca, New York, November 2000. See also "Administration Plans to Use Plum Island to Combat Terrorism," *The New York Times*, September 21, 1999.

an effective "first line of defense" against livestock pathogenic threats.[11]

Third, assessments of how to better foster more-coordinated and standardized links between the U.S. agricultural and intelligence communities should be undertaken. Although partnership agreements have been established between the USDA and the Defense Intelligence Agency (DIA), the Central Intelligence Agency (CIA), and the Federal Bureau of Investigation (FBI), they have yet to be embraced fully across the USDA, where only a small percentage of employees have the required clearances to access relevant security data.[12] Gauging the extent to which this intelligence gap needs to be bridged would provide a valuable (and necessary) base metric for the development of an effective and secure agroterrorist information-exchange environment.[13]

Fourth, attention needs to be focused on issues of law enforcement and criminal justice, particularly in the context of forensic investigations, to determine whether disease outbreaks have been deliberately orchestrated or are the result of naturally occurring phenomena. A useful USDA-FBI liaison program already exists, which allows for regular personnel exchanges and cross-agency meetings and discussions conducted in ad hoc working-group settings.[14] This framework of budding federal cooperation should be fully institutionalized and used to guide the establishment of similar arrangements at the state and local levels.

---

[11] This "force multiplier" function becomes especially important when one considers that APHIS—the USDA's main emergency management body—has a full-time staff of just 400, of which only 250 to 300 can realistically be expected to be available at any given time. (Author's interview with APHIS officials, Washington, D.C., July 1999. See also John Gordon and Steen Bech-Nielsen, "Biological Terrorism: A Direct Threat to Our Livestock Industry," *Military Medicine,* Vol. 151, No. 7, 1986, p. 357.)

[12] Author's interview with USDA official, Washington, D.C., July 1999.

[13] Parker (2002), p. 42.

[14] Comments made during the National Security Implications of Advances in Biotechnology: Threats to Plants and Animals planning meeting, National Academy of Sciences, Washington, D.C., August 1999.

Fifth, the overall effectiveness of the passive disease-reporting system needs to be revisited, especially in relation to providing more consistency with indemnity payments to compensate farmers for destroyed livestock.[15] In addition, steps should be taken to improve the effectiveness of farm emergency management communication channels, possibly through dedicated federal and state outreach and information programs. This type of systematic interaction could also be used to help elevate the level of trust between regulators and producers, particularly with regard to promoting the positive benefits of early disease reporting. The USDA is well placed to develop initiatives of this sort given the close links it has established with the American agribusiness spectrum through its extensive network of field offices, agricultural extension specialists, research facilities, and land-grant universities.[16]

Finally, surveillance, internal quality control, and emergency response at food processing facilities and packing plants need to be addressed and evaluated in terms of weighing the immediate costs against the long-term benefits of upgrading their biosecurity. Although ESA funding has been made available to support the oversight activities of the Food Safety and Inspection Services (FSIS), and full implementation of the Hazard Analysis and Critical Control Points (HACCP)[17] rule is now theoretically in place, the number of food processing and packing facilities that exist in the country relative to available federal and state inspectors largely precludes significant

---

[15] A proposed rule on FMD indemnity is currently in the works. At the time of this writing, however, no firm decision has been made on when or whether it would be enacted, or whether similar provisions would be introduced for other virulent and/or economically harmful animal diseases.

[16] Parker (2002), p. 32. According to Parker, the USDA is unique among federal agencies in its closeness to public and private constituencies.

[17] Under the HACCP rule, all facilities that slaughter and process meat and poultry are required to identify critical control points where microbial contamination is likely to occur and institute FSIS-designated systems to prevent or reduce the likelihood of it occurring. HACCP controls were instituted at the country's largest meat and poultry plants in January 1998 and have since been extended to all smaller facilities, including those with ten employees or fewer (comments made during the Annual Meeting of the American Public Health Association, Washington, D.C., November 18, 1998).

change in this area, at least on a uniform basis. A better alternative would be for the food processing companies themselves to assume responsibility for ensuring that their facilities meet basic, uniform requirements. Minimum common standards that should be followed across the industry include:

- Institution of more-effective site security, such as restricting individuals' entry and exit rights, locking up storage/bulk ingredient containers, and mounting video surveillance cameras at key internal processing hubs.
- More-thorough background checks of seasonal employees, including, at least, mandatory (and verified) character references. Medium-sized firms might also consider conducting basic security, criminal, and health background checks of workers involved in the manufacture of widely distributed and highly aggregated foodstuffs, such as sausage meat.
- The development of clearly documented, well-rehearsed product recall plans overseen by dedicated crisis management teams that are able to quickly assess the scope of potential problems and the procedures required for their containment and correction. At a minimum, all food processing companies should be able to produce the appropriate regulatory documents, as designated and prioritized by the Food and Drug Administration, in four hours or less on any day of the year for a given three-month time period.[18]

---

[18] These documents include:
- Complete label sets and ingredient lists for all products
- Process flow chart for each product
- Distribution lists (by product) for each day within the time period
- Written explanations of all commodity codes and expiration dates
- Monitoring and production logs and test results as required by the HACCP regulation system
- Complete current customer lists by state (including names, street addresses, and phone, fax, and pager numbers)
- Invoices and bills of lading for all ingredients
- Draft recall memos/letters to customers
- Draft recall press releases
- Draft recall verification/contact logs

Over the longer term, additional effort should be directed toward standardizing and streamlining food-supply and agricultural safety measures within the framework of a single, integrated strategy that cuts across the missions and capabilities of federal, state, and local agencies. An effort such as this would help to unify the patchwork of largely uncoordinated bio-emergency preparedness and response initiatives that presently exists in the United States. Integration of agriculture and food safety measures would also serve to reduce jurisdictional conflicts and eliminate unnecessary duplication of effort.

The components of such a strategic approach might include the elements listed in Table 4.1.

Implementing the various recommendations described in this chapter will require active political input and commitment. Reform along these lines will not be cheap and will definitely require federal backing. Considerable amounts of money have already been devoted to defending against the relatively low-risk scenario of viral attacks aimed at human populations. By comparison, contingency measures for livestock and crop protection have attracted only limited support, despite the comparative ease of carrying out such attacks and the implications they pose for the economic, social, and political stability of the United States. Serious assessments of the threat posed by biological terrorism suggest that this imbalance in federal backing needs to be modified, or at least recognized, as a matter of both fiscal responsibility and judicious public policy.

- Lists containing the names and numbers of primary and secondary contacts at all relevant regulatory agencies
- Logs and summaries of all consumer complaints for the time period in question
- Written plans for evaluating and deciding upon the scope of the recall
- Written plans for ensuring and maintaining a proper chain of command and control for all recalled products
- Written plans for the secure storage and/or destruction of all recalled products.

Details on these documents are from Jeff Farrar, "Foodborne Outbreak Investigations: What Agencies Do and What Regulators Expect of You," unpublished briefing given at California food-processing facilities, August 2000.

Table 4.1
Components of a National Strategy to Counter Biological Attacks Against Agriculture

Preventive Measures	Response Measures
Intelligence measures (identify potential threats and perpetrators; understand motivations; predict behavior)	Consequence management
Monitoring programs (detect and track specific pathogens and diseases)	Early detection of exotic/foreign pathogenic agents
Targeted BSL 4 research	Early prediction of disease dispersion patterns
International counterproliferation treaties, protocols, and agreements	Early containment procedures
Creation of agent-specific resistance in livestock	Epidemiology and treatment
Vaccination against specific List A agents	Depopulation and carcass disposal
Modification (where possible) of vulnerable U.S. food and agriculture practices	Diplomatic, legal, economic, and political responses
Biosecurity and surveillance	Compensation and indemnity
Education and training (federal, state, and local)	Education and training
	Public awareness and outreach programs
	Vaccine and pharmaceutical stockpiling

SOURCE: Most of the items in this list are from Parker (2002), pp. 40–41.

Bibliography

Books, Book Chapters, and Reports

Carus, Seth, *Bioterrorism and Biocrimes: The Illicit Use of Biological Agents in the 20th Century*, Center for Counterproliferation Research, Washington, D.C.: National Defense University, 1999.

Cole, L., *The Eleventh Plague: The Politics of Biological and Chemical Warfare*, New York: W.H. Freeman and Company, 1997.

Ekboir, Javier, *The Potential Impact of Foot and Mouth Disease in California: The Role and Contribution of Animal Health Surveillance and Monitoring Services*, Davis, Calif.: Agricultural Issues Center, 1999.

Jenkins, Brian, "Future Trends in International Terrorism," in Robert Slater and Michael Stohl (eds.), *Current Perspectives on International Terrorism*, London, UK: Macmillan Press, 1988.

Parker, Henry, *Agricultural Bioterrorism: A Federal Strategy to Meet the Threat*, McNair Paper 65, Washington, D.C.: Institute for National Strategic Studies, National Defense University, March 2002.

Purver, Ron, *Chemical and Biological Terrorism: A New Threat to Public Safety*, Conflict Studies 295, London, UK: Research Institute for the Study of Conflict and Terrorism, 1996/1997.

Regis, E., *The Biology of Doom: The History of America's Secret Germ Warfare Project*, New York: Henry Holt and Company, 1999.

Journal Articles

Brown, Corrie, "Impact and Risk of Foreign and Animal Diseases," *Vet Med Today*, Vol. 208, No. 7, p. 1039.

Garrett, Laurie, "The Return of Infectious Disease," *Foreign Affairs*, Vol. 75, No. 1, 1996.

Gordon, John, and Steen Bech-Nielsen, "Biological Terrorism: A Direct Threat to Our Livestock Industry," *Military Medicine*, Vol. 151, No. 7, 1986.

Gorman, Siobhan, "Bioterror Down on the Farm," *National Journal*, Vol. 27, July 1999.

Renlemann, C., and C. Spinelli, "An Economic Assessment of the Costs and Benefits of African Swine Fever Prevention," *Animal Health Insight*, Spring/Summer 1994.

Rogers, Paul, Simon Whitby, and Malcolm Dando, "Biological Warfare Against Crops," *Scientific American*, Vol. 280, No. 6, 1999.

Shell, Ellen, "Could Mad Cow Disease Happen Here?" *The Atlantic Monthly*, Vol. 282, No. 3, 1998.

Whitby, Simon, and Paul Rogers, "Anti-Crop Biological Warfare—Implications of the Iraqi and US Programs," *Defense Analysis*, Vol. 13, No. 3, 1997.

Official Reports, Briefings, and Testimony

Agricultural Research Service, *Agriculture's Defense Against Biological Warfare and Other Outbreaks*, Washington, D.C.: United States Department of Agriculture, 1961.

Agricultural Research Service, "Econoterrorism, a.k.a. Agricultural Bioterrorism or Asymmetric Use of Biological Weapons," unclassified briefing, Washington, D.C.: United States Department of Agriculture, February 28, 2000.

Chalk, Peter, "Terrorism, Infrastructure Protection, and the Agricultural Sector," testimony given before the Subcommittee on Oversight of Government Management, Restructuring and the District of Columbia, U.S. Senate, Washington, D.C., October 10, 2001.

Farrar, Jeff, "Foodborne Outbreak Investigations: What Agencies Do and What Regulators Expect of You," unpublished briefing given at California food-processing facilities, August 2000.

National Intelligence Council, *The Global Infectious Disease Threat and Its Implications for the United States*, National Intelligence Estimate 99-17D, Washington, D.C.: National Intelligence Council, January 2000.

Robinson, Robert, "Food Safety and Security," testimony given before the Subcommittee on Oversight of Government Management, Restructuring, and the District of Columbia of the Committee on Governmental Affairs, U.S. Senate, Washington, D.C., October 10, 2001.

Steele, Norm, *U.S. Agricultural Productivity, Concentration, and Vulnerability to Biological Weapons*, unclassified defense intelligence assessment briefing for the Department of Defense Futures Intelligence Program, Washington, D.C., January 14, 2000.

U.S. Department of Agriculture, *Advisory Committee on Agricultural Biotechnology*, Federal Register Notice 64, Washington, D.C.: USDA, n.d.

U.S. Department of Agriculture, *Agriculture—Farms, Acreage, and Foreign Trade: 1990–1998*, Washington, D.C.: National Agricultural Statistics Service, No. 1441, 1999.

The White House, *White Paper: The Clinton Administration's Policy on Critical Infrastructure Protection: Presidential Decision Directive 63*, Washington, D.C.: The White House, May 22, 1998.

Web-Based Sources

Animal and Plant Health Inspection Service, *National Veterinarian Accreditation Program (NVAP)* (available at http://www.aphis.usda.gov/vs/nvap/prt-text_data.html).

Bureau of Economic Analysis, "Gross Domestic Product: First Quarter 2002 (Advance)," (available at http://www.bea.doc.gov/bea/newsrel/gdp102a.htm).

Center for Infectious Disease Research and Policy, "Newcastle Disease Infiltrates Southern California Poultry Flocks," January 6, 2003 (available at http://www.cidrap.umn.edu/cidrap/content/biosecurity/ag-bio-sec/news/newcastle.html).

Office International des Epizooties, *Classification of Diseases* (available at http://www.oie.int/eng/maladies/en_classification.htm).

U.S. Department of Agriculture, *Budget Summary 2003* (available at http://www.usda.gov/agency/obpa/Budget-Summary/2003).

U.S. Department of Agriculture, *Foot and Mouth Disease Payment of Indemnity; Update of Provisions*, RIN 0597-AB34, November 2002 (available at http://frwebgate.access.gpo.gov).

Newspaper Articles, Magazine Articles, and News Releases

"Administration Plans to Use Plum Island to Combat Terrorism," *The New York Times*, September 21, 1999.

"After Foot and Mouth," *The Economist*, May 5, 2001.

"Agriculture Budget Proposes Increases in Key Areas," United States Department of Agriculture news release, No. 0031.02, February 4, 2002.

"Agro-Terrorism Still a Credible Threat," *The Wall Street Journal*, December 6, 2001.

"Eastern Oregon Farmers Ready to Eradicate Cattle Disease Threat," *The Oregonian*, August 17, 1999.

"Exotic Newcastle Disease Update," California Department of Food and Agriculture, Animal Health Branch, press release, October 15, 2003.

"Farmers Paid GBP1 Bn for Culled Animals," *The Daily Telegraph*, June 30, 2001.

"Fear and Breathing," *The Economist*, September 29, 2001.

"House Passes $4.6 Billion Bioterror Bill," *The Associated Press*, May 22, 2002.

"Malay Troops Slaughter Pigs in War on Virus," cnn.com International Web site, March 20, 1999.

"Pig-Borne Epidemic Kills 117," *The Sydney Morning Herald*, April 10, 1999.

"Plant Scientists Sound the Alarm on Agroterrorism," *The Philadelphia Inquirer*, September 13, 1999.

"Spring Returns to Rural Britain, But Not Tourists," *The Washington Post*, March 16, 2001.

"Stockgrowers Warned of Terrorism Threat," *The Chieftain*, August 19, 1999.

"This Wretched Cult of Blood and Money," *The Times*, May 23, 2001.

"Wonder Drugs at Risk," *The Washington Post*, April 19, 2001.

"The World's Newest Fear: Germ Warfare," *The Vancouver Sun*, September 24, 2001.

Other Sources

Neher, Nicholas, "Food Terrorism: The Need for a Coordinated Response—The Wisconsin Experience," unpublished position paper prepared for the United States Department of Agriculture's Agricultural Resource Management Division, n.d.

Rapoport, David, "Terrorists and Weapons of the Apocalypse," paper presented before the Future Developments in Terrorism conference, Cork, Ireland, March 1999.

Wilson, Terry, et al., "A Review of Agroterrorism, Biological Crimes, and Biological Warfare Targeting Agriculture," APHIS, Fort Detrick, Md., unpublished draft manuscript, 2001.

Made in the USA
Las Vegas, NV
27 December 2021

39433881R00037